For Felicity and Clemmie
R.D.

For Katie, Liza, Jamie
and Harriet
C.W.

The authors and publishers would like to thank the staff and pupils of Bousfield Primary School, South Bolton Gardens, London SW5 for their help in testing the recipes in this book.

Text © 1996 Roz Denny and Caroline Waldegrave

Illustrations © 1996 Jacky Paynter

Photographs © 1996 David Armstrong

Home Economist: Gina Steer

Stylist: Suzy Gittins

First published 1996
by Walker Books Ltd
87 Vauxhall Walk
London SE11 5HJ

Printed in Great Britain

This book has been typeset in ITC Garamond.

All rights reserved. No part of this publication may be reproduced in any form or by any means without permission.

ISBN 0-7445-5104-8

THE WALKER Children's FUN-TO-COOK BOOK

Roz Denny and Caroline Waldegrave

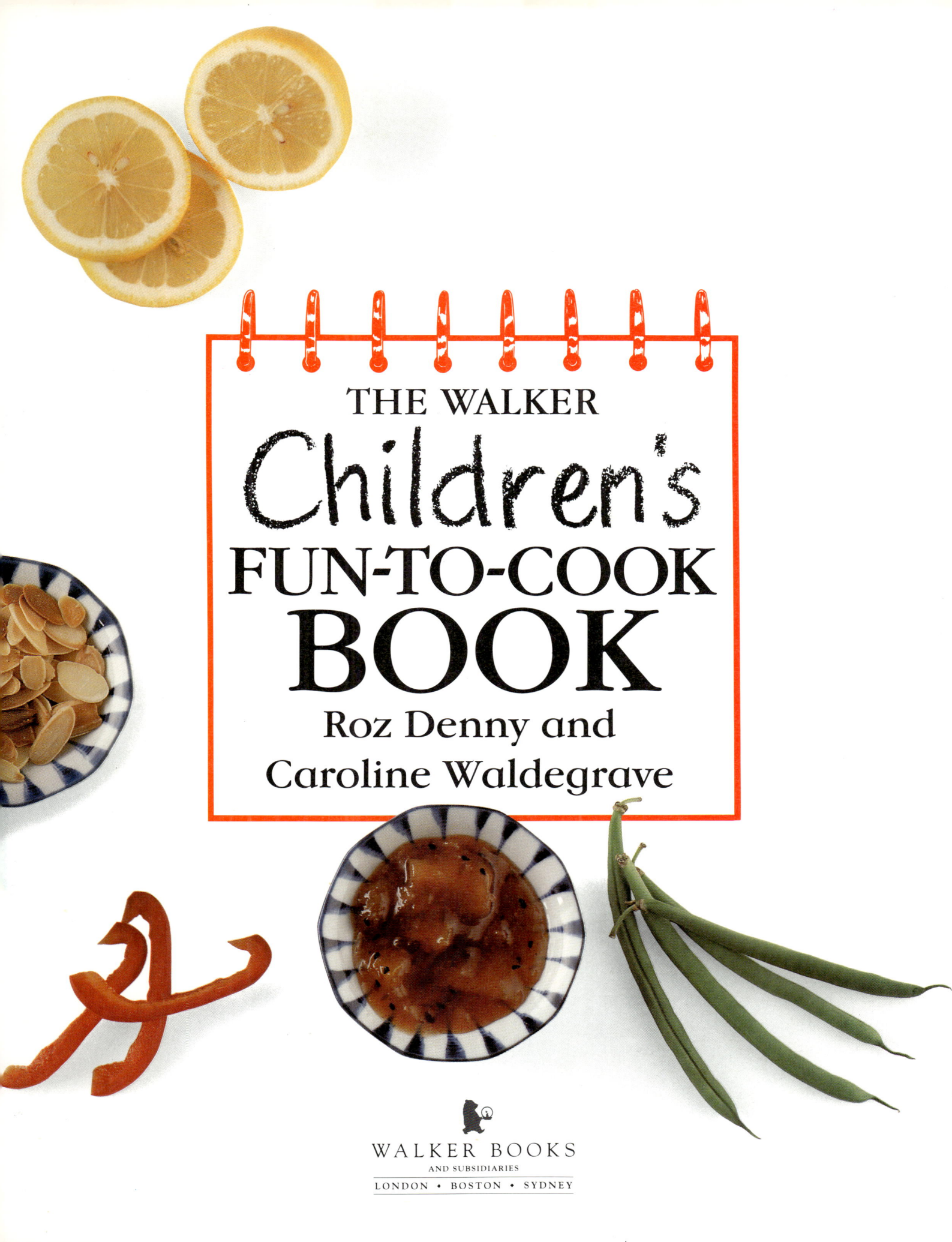

WALKER BOOKS
AND SUBSIDIARIES
LONDON · BOSTON · SYDNEY

Contents

Authors' note	7
Kitchen Information	8
Presentation	10
Basic Skills	12
Salade Tricolore	14
Sandwiches	16
Fish Dippers with Tomato Sauce	18
Baked Jacket Potatoes	20
Chicken Satay with Peanut Sauce	22
Turkey Pilaff	24
Vegetable and Bean Hotpot	26
Egg and Bacon Spaghetti	28
Cheese Omelette	30
Shepherd's Pie	32
Easy Breakfast Muffins	34
Orange Shortbread	36
Scones	38
Lemon Cake	40
Treacle Tart	42
Pavlova	44

Authors' Note

This is our second cookery book for children and as with the first all the recipes are fun to cook and easy to follow.

We believe that if you eat a well-balanced diet now, when you are young, the habit will stay with you for the rest of your life. A balanced diet should include plenty of fresh fruit and vegetables, cereals, pasta, rice and bread. Try not to have too many foods that are high in sugar and fat like cakes, biscuits, crisps, sweets, chocolates and fried foods. Of course there is no harm in having special treats from time to time and this book includes delicious recipes for cakes and desserts as well as more healthy dishes.

Many of the recipes are simple, like scones, muffins and sandwiches. Some recipes, like Shepherd's Pie and Pavlova, are more complicated but will help you to practise and improve your cookery techniques. We have also included a page of basic skills to help you, so read all the introductory pages carefully before you start.

If you are an experienced cook you might like to try cooking and serving a whole meal. We have included some useful hints on presentation to help you serve your meal properly.

We do hope that you have fun cooking and enjoy eating all these dishes. The recipes have been tested by lots of children and we would particularly like to thank the staff and children of Bousfield School whose help was invaluable in the preparation of this book.

Roz and Caroline

Kitchen Information

Before you start

- ★ Put on your apron and tie your hair back if you need to.
- ★ Wash your hands.
- ★ Read the recipe. Collect all the ingredients and equipment you need.
- ★ Check whether you need to turn on the grill or oven.

While you are cooking

- ★ When you are cooking over heat and taking things out of the oven always wear oven gloves.
- ★ When using a knife never cut towards your hands.
- ★ Always cut on a chopping board.
- ★ Follow the recipe step by step.

When you've finished

- ★ Don't forget to do the washing up!
- ★ Put all the ingredients away.
- ★ Clean all the surfaces with a hot soapy dishcloth.
- ★ Check you have switched off the oven, rings and grill.

Tips on measuring

How to measure syrup
Warm a metal tablespoon in a mug of hot water. Spoon the syrup from the tin. It should run off easily.

A pinch of salt
When cooks talk about a "pinch" of salt, they mean the amount you can hold between your thumb and your first finger.

Measuring with spoons
When you measure with spoons they should be level rather than heaped. You can buy metric measuring spoons which are easy to use and very accurate.

Be hygienic as you cook

- ★ Wash your hands before and during cooking.
- ★ Wash all fruit and vegetables.
- ★ Always use clean tea towels.
- ★ Never use the same cloth to wipe the work surface and the floor!
- ★ Never taste with your fingers.
- ★ Keep pets out of the kitchen if you can.
- ★ Germs like warmth, moisture and time to grow and multiply, so give them cold, dry conditions and no time to increase.
- ★ Try not to keep food warm for more than half an hour.

Managing your fridge

- ★ Keep it cold (5°C or colder).
- ★ Never leave the door open longer than necessary.
- ★ Never put hot or warm food into the fridge.
- ★ Do not allow raw food (e.g. meat or fish) to touch cooked food or food that is to be eaten without cooking (e.g. salad or cream cakes).

Words cooks use

Beat
Stir ingredients together briskly until smooth and creamy.
Boil
Bring water to boiling point so it bubbles and gives off steam.
Chop
Cut into small even pieces.
Core
Cut out the seeds and central core of vegetables or fruit.
Dissolve
Let a solid ingredient such as gelatine or sugar melt in liquid.
Garnish
Add herbs or salad to decorate a savoury dish.
Knead
Rub bread dough backwards and forwards on a board to make the dough smooth.

Make a well
Form a hole in the middle of a bowl of flour with a spoon.
Marinate
To soak in a marinade of liquids or flavourings, to flavour or tenderize.
Mash
Break up foods until smooth using a fork or potato masher.
Peel
Take off the outer skin of vegetables or fruit with a vegetable peeler or small cook's knife.
Prove
Leave uncooked bread dough to rise a second time before cooking.
Rubbing-in
Rub fat into flour using your thumb and forefinger until the mixture looks like coarse breadcrumbs.
Season
Add salt and pepper to taste.

Shred
Cut into thin strands by slicing a stack of leaves.
Simmer
Keep water hot, so it bubbles gently but does not boil.
Slice
Cut into long pieces or rings, thick or thin.
Soften
Leave butter or cream cheese at room temperature so it will beat more easily.
Stir fry
Cook quickly, ideally in a wok, turning the food constantly so that it is cooked and crisp.
Whisk
Beat with metal whisk to lighten the mixture with air.

Conversion charts

The conversions are not exact equivalents. Never mix metric and imperial measures in a recipe! If you do, the proportions may be wrong.

Solids		Liquids	
15 g	½ oz	15 ml	½ fl oz (1 tablespoon)
25 g	1 oz	30 ml	1 fl oz (2 tablespoons)
40 g	1½ oz	45 ml	1½ fl oz (3 tablespoons)
50 g	2 oz	60 ml	2 fl oz
65 g	2½ oz	75 ml	2 fl oz
75 g	3 oz	90 ml	3 fl oz
100 g	3½ oz	100 ml	3 fl oz
125 g	4 oz	125 ml	4 fl oz
150 g	5 oz	150 ml	5 fl oz (¼ pint)
175 g	6 oz	175 ml	6 fl oz
200 g	7 oz	200 ml	7 fl oz
250 g	8 oz	250 ml	8 fl oz
300 g	10 oz	300 ml	10 fl oz (½ pint)
375 g	12 oz	350 ml	12 fl oz
425 g	14 oz	400 ml	14 fl oz
500 g	1 lb	450 ml	15 fl oz (¾ pint)
		500 ml	18 fl oz
		600 ml	20 fl oz/ (1 pint)

Oven temperatures

Gas Mark	Centigrade	Fahrenheit
¼	110°C	225°F
½	130°C	250°F
1	140°C	275°F
2	150°C	300°F
3	160°C	325°F
4	180°C	350°F
5	190°C	375°F
6	200°C	400°F
7	220°C	425°F
8	230°C	450°F

All ovens are different and cooking times are only a guide. Get into the habit of touching and looking at food to find out if it is properly cooked.

 When you see a red square like this in a recipe, always ask an adult to help you.

Presentation

If you have spent a long time cooking and preparing a meal, it seems a shame not to present it properly.

How to Lay a Table

It does not matter very much where you position all the knives and forks but this is one suggestion.

The knives, forks and spoons are arranged in such a way that those to be used first are on the outside. Always lay a side plate and arrange the napkin on it; simply fold it in half or try folding it like the one below.

Food Presentation

★ **Keep it simple**
Try not to overdecorate food or it can begin to look messy.

★ **Keep it fresh**
Try not to arrange food too far in advance. It will start to look tired.

★ **Height in the centre**
Arrange the food on a plate so that there is a bit of height in the centre.

★ **Look generous**
A plate of food should look full but not clumsy.

★ **Stick to your plan**
Once you have arranged the food, don't change your mind! It always looks a mess if you do.

To Fold a Napkin

Napkins for folding should be quite large – about 60 cm square. Choose good quality paper ones if you are unable to borrow well-starched cotton or linen ones.

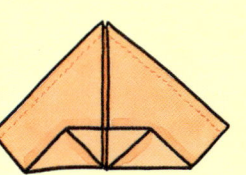

5. Fold the same point down to the base.

6. Turn the napkin over.

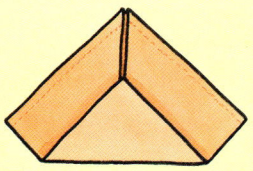

1. Lay the napkin out flat.
2. Fold into a triangle.
3. Fold up the two bottom corners.
4. Fold the bottom point two thirds of the way up.

  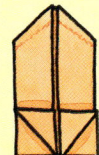 

7. Fold one third of the napkin across.
8. Tuck the other side into the bottom fold.
9. Turn it over and fold the central point down.
10. Stand it up and fold down the top corners.

Basic Skills

Shortcrust Pastry

Crumbly pastry is hard to handle, but it tastes much nicer once baked than pastry that is wet and easier to handle.

Makes 300 g of pastry

You will need:
200 g plain flour
pinch of salt
30 g lard or vegetable shortening
70 g butter or margarine
very cold water

1 Sift the flour with the salt into a mixing bowl. Cut the lard and butter into 1 cm cubes and add to the flour.

2 Rub the fat into the flour with your fingertips. Lift your hands high and drop the fat back into the bowl to trap air.

3 When the mixture looks like coarse breadcrumbs, add 2 to 3 tablespoons of water. You may need to add more.

4 Mix to a firm ball of dough. Wrap the dough completely in clingfilm and chill for 30 minutes before using.

To Chop an Onion

Once they are peeled, onions can be slippery and hard to chop, so use your knife very carefully.

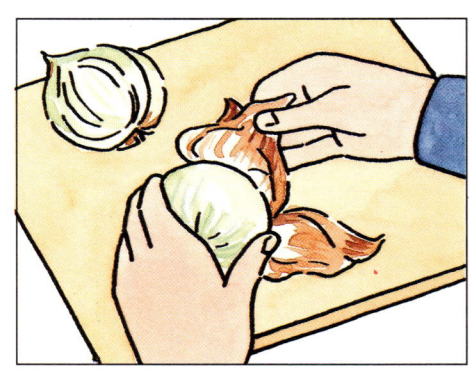

1 Slice the onion lengthwise through the core. Peel both halves. Do not remove the root.

2 Put one half on the chopping board. With a sharp knife make a series of parallel cuts down.

To Separate an Egg

Sometimes you will need just egg yolks or just egg whites for a recipe. This is how you separate one from the other.

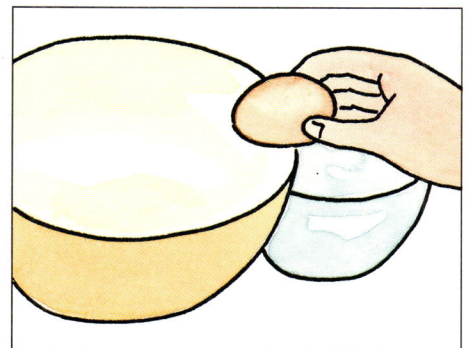

1 You will need 2 clean bowls. Hold the egg in one hand and crack it sharply across the middle against one of the bowls.

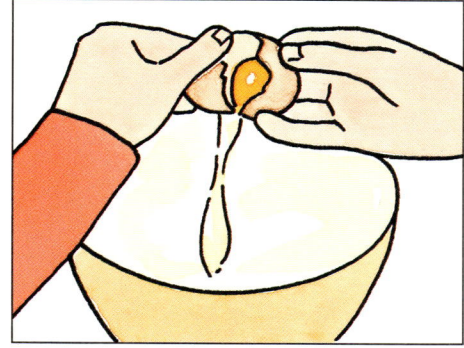

2 Gently pull the shell apart, keeping the yolk in one half and letting the white fall into the bowl.

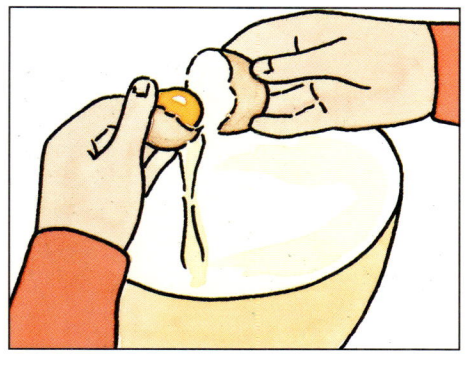

3 Carefully tip the yolk from one half-shell to the other, letting the rest of the white drop into one of the bowls.

4 Use the broken edge of the empty shell to cut off any white that won't fall. Drop the yolk into the other bowl.

5 If you need to separate more eggs, use two bowls per egg in case you make a mistake, and add them together.

3 Make a series of cuts at right angles to the previous set to chop the onion into little pieces.

To Make Fresh Breadcrumbs

One slice of bread makes about 1tbsp or 25 g of breadcrumbs. The bread should be about 4 days old. Cut the crusts off and chop finely in a food processor.

To Grate the Zest of Fruit

The zest of an orange or lemon is just the coloured part of the skin. Wash the fruit and grate it on the finest holes of the grater. Take care not to grate the white pith. Be careful of your fingers.

Salade Tricolore

Red, white and green are the colours of this simple Mediterranean salad. Serve it with crusty bread to mop up the delicious juices.

Serves 4

> You will need:
> 2 large tomatoes
> 2 tablespoons olive oil
> 75 g Mozzarella cheese
> 12 small fresh basil leaves
> sea salt
> ground black pepper

1 Using a serrated knife, slice the tops off the tomatoes as thinly as possible and throw them away.

2 Cut the tomatoes into thin slices and lay them on a round plate, sprinkling in between with salt and pepper.

3 Drizzle half the oil evenly over the tomatoes and tuck some of the fresh basil leaves between the pieces.

4 Cover with clingfilm and chill in the fridge for 1 to 2 hours, until some juice starts to come out of the tomatoes.

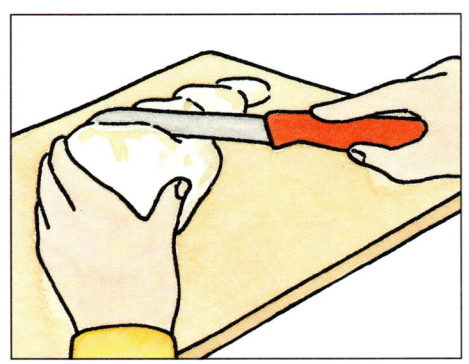

5 Cut the Mozzarella into thin slices with the knife. Uncover the tomatoes and scatter the cheese on top.

6 Trickle over the rest of the oil. Season with more salt and pepper and garnish with the rest of the basil.

Sandwiches

Sandwiches can be made using lots of different types of bread – rolls, sliced white or brown, or baguettes. The principle is basically the same.

Egg and Cress

2 hard-boiled eggs
3 tablespoons mayonnaise
1 punnet mustard and cress
salt and pepper

Tuna Fish and Spring Onion

200 g can tuna fish
3 tablespoons mayonnaise
4 spring onions
salt and pepper

Cucumber

It is best to use sliced bread for cucumber sandwiches rather than baguettes or rolls.

¼ cucumber
salt

Making sandwiches

★ Use softened butter and spread it evenly over the surface of the bread.

★ Use plenty of filling. These quantities are enough for 6 small rolls, 3 rounds of sandwiches or 1 medium size baguette.

★ If you are using unsliced bread spread the butter on the loaf before slicing it.

★ Sandwiches made from sliced bread should have their crusts removed and be cut into quarters.

1 Peel the eggs very carefully. Wash them under cold running water and then dry them well on absorbent kitchen paper.

2 On a chopping board, chop the eggs up quite finely. Put into a bowl and add the mayonnaise. Mix gently.

3 Snip the tops off the mustard and cress and mix with the eggs and mayonnaise. Season with salt and pepper.

1 Drain the tin of tuna fish in a sieve placed over a bowl. Measure out the mayonnaise into another bowl.

2 Wash the spring onions. Cut off the green part and the roots. Chop fairly roughly and add to the mayonnaise.

3 Add the tuna fish to the mayonnaise and spring onions and mix everything together well. Season to taste.

1 Peel the cucumber and slice it as thinly as you can. Put it into a sieve and sprinkle it with salt. Leave for 20 minutes.

2 Rinse the cucumber thoroughly under running cold water and then drain the pieces well on kitchen paper.

3 Divide the cucumber evenly between the slices of bread and press down firmly before cutting off crusts and slicing.

Fish Dippers with Tomato Sauce

Make your own fish fingers!

Serves 4

You will need:
4 plaice or sole fillets
salt and pepper
1 egg
1 teaspoon dried mixed herbs
100 g natural colour dried breadcrumbs
2 teaspoons ground paprika
about 200 ml oil for frying
TO SERVE:
1 lemon, cut into quarters
fresh sprigs of parsley
SAUCE:
2 tablespoons mayonnaise
4 tablespoons tomato ketchup

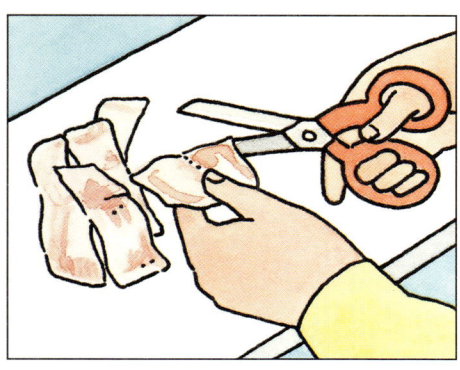

1 Using kitchen scissors, cut the fish into long strips across the grain. Season with salt and pepper.

2 Break the egg into a shallow bowl. Add the mixed herbs and beat with a fork. Mix in the fish strips.

3 Put the breadcrumbs and paprika into a plastic food bag. Add 3 or 4 strips of fish and gently shake the bag to coat.

4 Lay the coated strips on a large plate. Repeat with the rest of the fish, just coating a few pieces at a time.

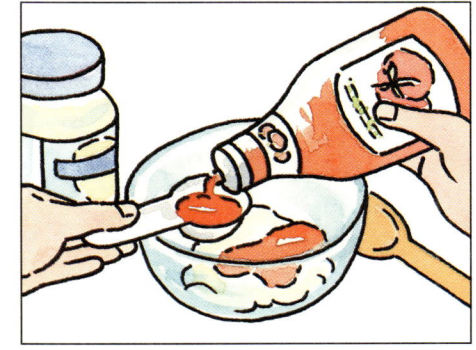

5 Chill the fish in the fridge for about an hour, to "set" the crumbs. Mix the mayonnaise and ketchup together.

6 Heat the oil in a deep frying pan for 3 to 5 minutes. It is hot enough when a cube of bread browns in 30 seconds.

7 Carefully place a few of the strips into the oil with a fish slice. Cook for 2 or 3 minutes, turning once, until golden.

8 Remove with the fish slice and drain on kitchen towels. Fry the rest of the fish, reheating the oil in between.

9 Serve on a plate with the lemon quarters and garnish with parsley. Serve the tomato sauce in a small dish.

Baked Jacket Potatoes

Choose one of the three tasty fillings shown here. Each of these recipes makes enough filling for 4 potatoes.

Serves 4

You will need:
4 baking potatoes, washed
a little olive or sunflower oil
TOPPINGS:
Soured Cream
142 ml carton soured cream
a packet fresh dill sprigs
1 spring onion
2 teaspoons poppy seeds
salt and pepper
Bean and Cheese
220 g can beans in tomato sauce
50 g Bavarian smoked cheese or smoked Cheddar
Tuna and Corn
2 tablespoons soft cheese
1 tablespoon milk
2 tablespoons sweetcorn
100 g can tuna fish

Preheat the oven to Gas Mark 5, 190°C, 375°F

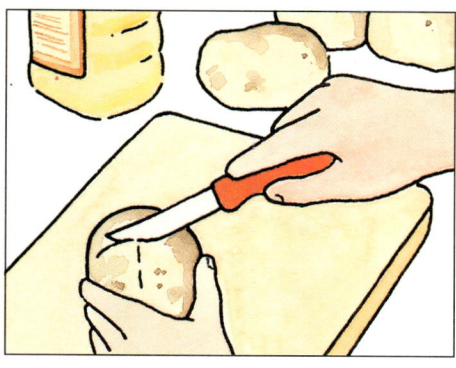

1 Using a sharp knife, score a cross on the top of each potato. Pour a little oil into your hands and rub it into each one.

2 Put the potatoes on a baking sheet and bake for about 1 hour until they are soft inside. Make your filling while you wait.

3 Soured Cream
Beat the cream until smooth. Snip the dill and onion into the cream and add the poppy seeds.

4 Bean and Cheese
Drain some of the liquid off the beans. Put in a bowl. Cut the cheese into cubes. Mix with the beans.

5 Tuna and Corn
Beat the cheese until smooth. Add the milk. Drain the corn and tuna and mix into the cheese.

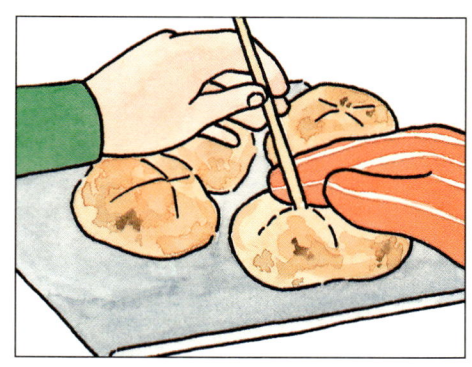

6 Use a skewer to check that the potatoes are cooked. They should feel soft in the middle. Remove with oven gloves.

7 Cut the potatoes along the crosses and, using oven gloves, push up the flesh from the base.

8 Spoon your prepared filling over the pushed-up potato and serve immediately while still hot.

Baking Potatoes in a Microwave

You can bake potatoes in a microwave oven. Prepare potatoes as for step 1 and place on a plate. Cook on full power for 5 minutes for one potato, 7 minutes for two potatoes and up to 12 minutes for three potatoes.

(These are timings for a 650 watt, category B oven. Check the instruction book if yours is different.)

Chicken Satay with Peanut Sauce

Vegetarians can use cubes of tofu instead of chicken. If possible, use wooden satay sticks but remember to soak them in cold water before you start.

Makes 6 kebabs

You will need:
- 250 g skinless chicken breasts or 285 g pack tofu, preferably smoked
- 6 small bamboo satay sticks or small metal skewers
- 3 or 4 lettuce leaves

MARINADE:
- 4 spring onions
- 2 cm piece fresh root ginger
- 1 clove garlic
- 1 teaspoon ground coriander
- 1 teaspoon ground cumin
- 2 tablespoons light soy sauce
- 1 tablespoon sunflower oil
- 1 tablespoon lemon juice
- 1 teaspoon sugar

PEANUT SAUCE:
- 2 tablespoons peanut butter
- 6 tablespoons water
- 2 teaspoons soy sauce
- 1 teaspoon sugar
- 1 teaspoon lemon juice

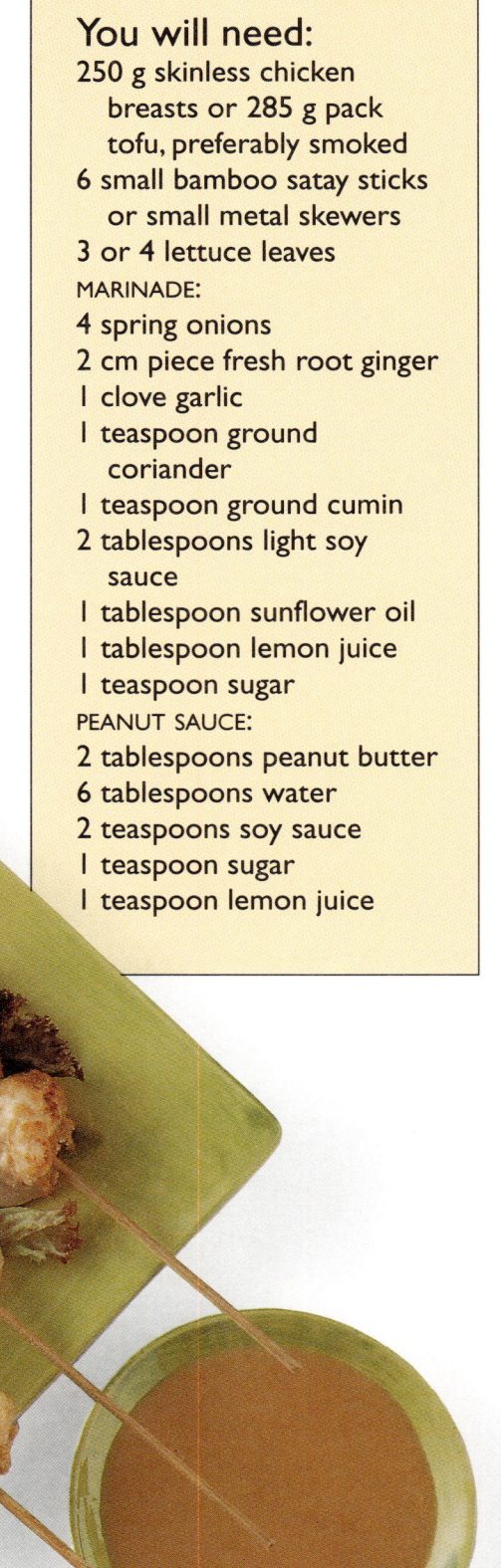

1 On a chopping board, cut the chicken breasts or tofu into bite size cubes, about 2 cm square.

2 Trim the onions and cut into small pieces. Peel the ginger and grate on the small holes of the grater. Crush in the garlic.

3 Add the rest of the marinade ingredients and mix in the chicken or tofu. Cover and leave in the fridge for 1 hour.

4 Meanwhile, make the sauce. Put the peanut butter, water, soy sauce, sugar and lemon juice into a small saucepan.

5 Bring to the boil, stirring until smooth. Simmer for 2 minutes and pour into a small serving bowl to cool.

6 Roll the lettuce all together and cut into shreds with a sharp knife. Put it on to a serving plate and leave to one side.

7 Drain the wooden satay sticks if you are using them and thread about 6 pieces of chicken or tofu on to each one.

8 Preheat a grill until hot, put the satays under, then turn down to medium. Cook for 5 minutes on each side.

9 Carefully place the satays on the plate lined with shredded lettuce, and serve with the sauce.

Turkey Pilaff

Use the fragrant basmati rice for this dish. It has more natural flavour.

Serves 4

You will need:
- 250 g basmati rice
- 1 chopped onion (see page 12)
- 1 small red or yellow pepper
- 125 g whole green beans
- 2 cloves garlic
- 4 tablespoons sunflower oil
- about 250 g turkey stir fry strips or skinless chicken breasts cut in slices
- 2 to 3 teaspoons mild curry powder
- 900 ml chicken stock, already made
- 2 teaspoons mango chutney
- 150 g pot natural yogurt
- flaked and toasted almonds
- salt and pepper

1 Rinse the rice in a sieve under a cold tap until the water runs clear. Leave the rice to drain over a bowl.

2 Wipe the pepper, halve it, remove the core and shake out the seeds. Cut into strips and then into small pieces.

3 Cut the tops and tails off the beans and slice into chunks. Peel the garlic and place ready in a garlic crusher.

4 Heat half the oil in a saucepan and stir fry the meat for 2 minutes. Remove with a slotted spoon, and set aside.

5 Heat the remaining oil in the pan. Add the onion and pepper, then crush in the garlic. Stir and cook for 2 minutes.

6 Carefully add the rice – it might hiss a bit. Stir well and fry gently for about 2 minutes, then mix in the curry powder.

7 Stir in the stock, chutney and beans, then season. Return the meat, bring to the boil, then lower to a simmer.

8 Cover the pan and cook for 10 minutes, then uncover and simmer for 2 minutes. Remove the pan and let it stand.

9 Carefully stir with a fork and taste to check the seasoning. Serve hot, topped with yogurt and toasted almonds.

Vegetable and Bean Hotpot

A great meat-free main meal that is tasty and wholesome.

Serves 3 to 4

You will need:
- 2 medium size leeks
- 2 carrots
- 1 red pepper
- 125 g button mushrooms
- 3 tablespoons olive oil
- 2 tablespoons wholemeal flour
- 400 g can chopped tomatoes
- 150 ml stock or water
- 432 g can mixed pulses or red kidney beans
- ½ teaspoon dried thyme
- 2 bay leaves
- 3 medium size potatoes
- 25 g butter, melted
- salt and pepper

Preheat the oven to Gas Mark 5, 190°C, 375°F

1 Trim the leeks, then cut into thick slices. Wash well in a colander. Peel the carrots and cut into slices or sticks.

2 Halve the pepper, remove the core and shake out the seeds, then cut into slices. Cut the mushrooms in half.

4 Stir in the flour, then add the tomatoes, stock and the liquid from the beans. Bring to the boil and add the herbs.

5 Season to taste, simmer for about 5 minutes, then add the beans. Pour into a medium size casserole dish.

6 Peel the potatoes and cut into very thin slices. Arrange these on top of the casserole in overlapping circles.

3 Heat the oil in a large saucepan and fry the leeks, carrots, pepper and mushrooms for about 5 minutes until softened.

7 Brush with melted butter and bake uncovered for an hour, or until the potatoes are golden and crisp.

Egg and Bacon Spaghetti

You can use any pasta for this. Just follow the cooking times on the packet.

Serves 2 to 3

You will need:
2 large (size 2) eggs
200 g spaghetti
125 g rindless streaky bacon
parsley sprigs, to fill a teacup
1 tablespoon butter
a whole nutmeg
2 teaspoons olive or sunflower oil
1 tablespoon wine vinegar
3 tablespoons grated Parmesan cheese
salt and pepper

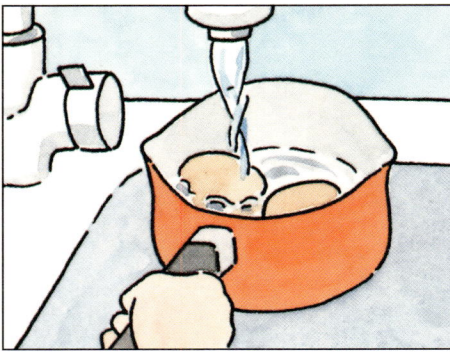

1 Place the eggs in a small saucepan and cover with cold water. Bring to the boil, then simmer for 10 minutes.

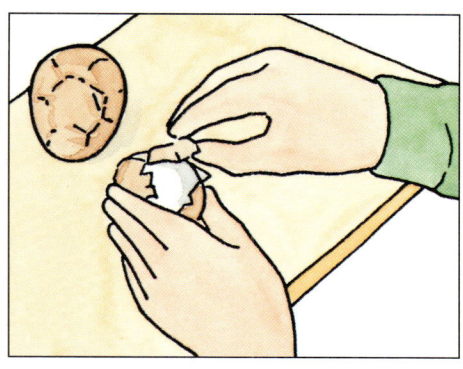

2 Drain carefully and run the eggs under cold water to cool, then tap the shells all over and peel as neatly as possible.

3 Rinse the peeled eggs and carefully cut them into slices with an egg slicer or a knife on a chopping board.

4 Cut the bacon into short strips with kitchen scissors and set aside. Then snip the parsley into the cup.

5 Bring a large pan of water to the boil, then add the spaghetti, pushing the strands down with a spoon as they soften.

6 Boil according to the instructions on the packet (usually about 5 to 10 minutes). Turn the heat down if it boils over.

7 Heat the oil in a pan and fry the bacon until crisp. Turn the heat off and add the vinegar carefully, as it will froth.

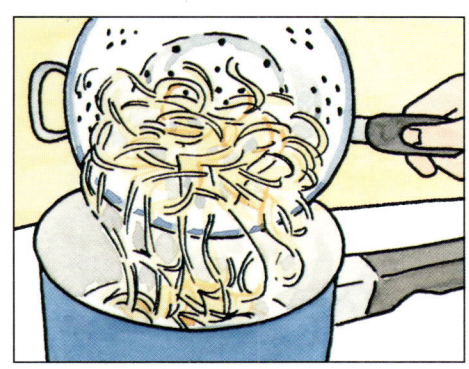

8 When the pasta is cooked, stand a colander in the sink and carefully tip it in to drain. Tip it back immediately.

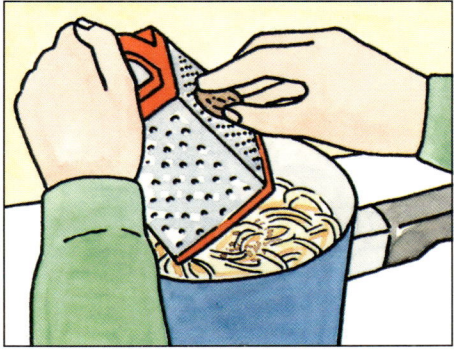

9 Toss in the butter and carefully grate in about a quarter of the nutmeg, using the fine holes of a grater.

10 Add the bacon and parsley to the pasta, season, and then divide between 2 or 3 plates. Top with the egg and Parmesan.

Cheese Omelette

Before you make the omelette read the recipe carefully. Omelettes should be eaten as soon as they are made so you must be completely organized before you start to cook.

Makes 1 omelette

You will need:
3 eggs
1 tablespoon cold water
large knob of butter
20 g grated Cheddar cheese
salt and pepper
TO SERVE:
washed and shredded lettuce
halved cherry tomatoes

1 Break the eggs into a bowl and whisk lightly with a fork. Mix in the water and salt and pepper to taste.

2 Melt the butter in a heavy frying pan, swirling the butter around to coat the bottom and sides of the pan.

3 When the butter stops foaming, pour the eggs into the pan. Move the pan gently back and forth on the heat.

4 As the mixture sets at the edges, use a fish slice to push the set omelette towards the middle very gently.

5 At the same time, tilt the pan slightly so that runny egg from the middle replaces the set omelette.

6 When the omelette is set on the bottom but still creamy on the top, sprinkle the grated cheese over one half.

7 With a fork or fish slice fold the half of the omelette not covered with cheese over on to the cheesy side.

8 Carefully lift up the frying pan and slide the omelette on to a plate. Serve immediately, while still hot.

Shepherd's Pie

This takes quite a long time to make but you can make it one day and reheat it the next.

Serves 4 to 6

You will need:

FOR THE MEAT SAUCE:
650 g lean minced beef
1 tablespoon oil
1 onion, finely chopped (see page 12)
1 carrot, finely chopped
1 stick celery, finely chopped
2 teaspoons flour
300 ml water
1 bay leaf
Worcestershire sauce (if you like it)
1 tablespoon tomato ketchup
salt and pepper

FOR THE MASHED POTATO:
700 g potatoes, peeled
150 ml milk
25 g butter
salt and pepper
15 g extra butter

1 Heat the oil in a frying pan. When it is really hot, add a third of the meat and fry until lightly browned.

2 When the meat is cooked, remove with a slotted spoon and put it in a saucepan. Repeat with the other two thirds.

3 Fry the onion, carrot and celery in the frying pan until soft and brown. Add the vegetables to the mince in the pan.

4 Add the flour to the saucepan and stir well over the heat for one minute. Add the water and bring to the boil.

5 Add the rest of the ingredients and simmer gently for 45 minutes. Add more water if it starts to look dry.

6 Preheat the oven to Gas Mark 6, 200°C, 400°F. Cut the potatoes into even chunks and boil them for 10 to 15 minutes.

7 Drain the potatoes through a colander in the sink, then return them to the saucepan and mash over a gentle heat.

8 Push the potato to one side of the pan, pour the milk into the other side and heat the milk until it bubbles.

9 When the milk is nearly boiling, add the butter and then beat into the potato. Season to taste with salt and pepper.

10 Remove the bay leaf, then tip the mince into a pie dish. If it is very wet, spoon off some of the gravy. Cool for 10 minutes.

11 Spoon the potato over the mince and spread it flat, making a pattern on top with a fork. Dot with knobs of butter.

12 Using oven gloves, put the pie in the oven and bake for about 45 minutes, until the top is golden brown.

Easy Breakfast Muffins

You can weigh the ingredients out the night before you plan to have these muffins, then just mix and bake in the morning. Eat them while they are still warm.

Makes 12 muffins

You will need:
- 200 g self-raising flour
- 1 teaspoon ground cinnamon
- 40 g soft brown sugar
- 50 g raisins or chocolate chips
- 1 (size 3) egg
- 250 ml milk
- 2 tablespoons sunflower oil
- 12 paper baking cases

Preheat the oven to Gas Mark 5, 190°C, 375°F

1 Put the flour and cinnamon into a sieve, then stir them into a large mixing bowl below to sift out any lumps.

2 Mix in the brown sugar and raisins, or chocolate chips. Break up any lumps in the sugar with your fingertips.

3 Break the egg into a jug and beat it with a fork. Then add the milk and the oil. Beat again until well mixed.

4 When you are ready to bake, put 12 large paper baking cases into a 12 hole bun tin, ideally with deep, straight sides.

5 Quickly stir the two mixtures together but be careful not to overbeat. It doesn't matter if you can still see some flour.

6 Spoon into the paper cases and bake for 15 minutes until risen and brown. Remove from the oven with oven gloves.

Orange Shortbread

Shortbread is particularly delicious if it is made with ground rice.

You will need:
100 g softened butter
50 g caster sugar
grated zest of 2 oranges
(see page 13)
100 g plain flour
50 g ground rice

Preheat the oven to Gas Mark 3, 160°C, 325°F

1 Put the butter into a mixing bowl. Stand the bowl on a damp cloth to stop it slipping and beat the butter until soft.

2 Add the orange zest and beat lightly. Add the sugar and beat again until the mixture is very soft and creamy.

3 Sift the flour and ground rice into the bowl and mix quickly but lightly to a smooth paste. Don't worry if it is a bit dry.

4 Place a small flan ring on a baking sheet and press the paste into it. Remove ring and flatten with a rolling pin.

5 If you do not have a flan ring, just press the paste on to a baking sheet and shape it into a 16 cm circle.

6 Prick lightly with a fork and then mark into 8 wedges with a knife. Sprinkle lightly with a little extra caster sugar.

7 Bake in the middle of the oven for 30 to 35 minutes until it is a pale biscuit colour. Leave to cool for 5 minutes.

8 Lift the shortbread on to a wire rack to cool completely. When it is cold, carefully break into the marked wedges.

Scones

For a traditional Devon tea serve these scones while still warm, with butter, whipped or clotted cream and raspberry jam.

Makes 6 to 8

You will need:
250 g self-raising flour
½ teaspoon salt
50 g butter
25 g caster sugar
150 ml milk

Preheat the oven to Gas Mark 7, 220°C, 425°F

1 Sift the flour with the salt into a mixing bowl. Cut the butter into small chunks and add it to the flour and salt.

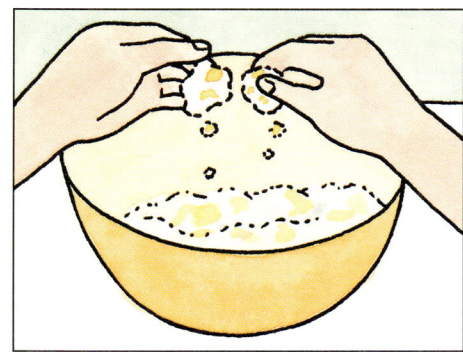

2 Rub in the butter using your fingertips until the mixture looks like coarse breadcrumbs. Then stir in the sugar.

3 Make a big well in the middle of the flour and pour in the milk. Mix with a palette knife to make a spongy dough.

4 Tip the dough on to a floured worktop. It should be handled as little as possible, so knead until it is just smooth.

5 Roll the dough out until it is 2.5 cm thick and stamp out scones with a small fluted cutter. Re-roll and use the trimmings.

6 Carefully place the scones on a lightly floured baking sheet and sprinkle each one with a little extra flour.

7 Put the baking tray in the oven and bake the scones for 7 to 8 minutes until well risen and golden brown.

8 Remove from the oven, using oven gloves, and lift the scones on to a wire rack, with a fish slice, to cool.

Variations:

Cheese Scones:
Leave out half the butter and all of the sugar. When you have rubbed in the 25 g butter, add 25 g of grated Cheddar cheese and then carry on from step 3.

Raisin Scones:
(see left)
Add 25 g of raisins when you add the sugar and then carry on from step 3.

Lemon Cake

This is a deliciously moist cake that is ideal for picnics and lunch boxes.

You will need:
- 150 g softened butter
- 150 g caster sugar
- 2 eggs
- grated zest of 1 lemon (see page 13)
- 150 g self-raising flour
- 4 tablespoons milk
- 2 tablespoons icing sugar
- juice of 1 lemon

Preheat the oven to Gas Mark 4, 180°C, 350°F

1 Put the butter into a mixing bowl. Stand the bowl on a damp cloth to stop it slipping and beat the butter until soft.

2 Add the caster sugar and beat again. Break each egg into a mug, then put them together and beat well with a fork.

3 Gradually add the beaten eggs to the butter and sugar mixture. Do not add them too fast as the mixture may curdle.

4 Beat in the lemon zest and then sift in the flour. Add enough milk to make the mixture of dropping consistency.

5 Spoon the mixture into a 900 g non-stick loaf tin and spread it flat with a spatula. Bake for 40 minutes.

6 Wearing oven gloves, test the top of the cake. If it is springy it is cooked. If not, bake for 5 more minutes.

7 Mix the icing sugar with the lemon juice. Prick the top of the cake with a fork and pour the juice over while still warm.

8 Leave the cake to cool in the tin for 15 minutes then carefully turn it out and leave to cool completely on a wire rack.

41

Treacle Tart

If making shortcrust pastry takes too long you can buy a 300 g packet of ready made pastry for this recipe.

You will need:
1 quantity shortcrust pastry (see page 12)
flour for dusting
4 tablespoons fresh white breadcrumbs (see page 13)
grated zest and juice of 1 lemon (see page 13)
pinch of ground ginger
a tin of golden syrup

Preheat the oven to Gas Mark 5, 190°C or 375°F

1 Dust the work surface with flour and roll the pastry out. Use short even strokes and turn to stop it sticking.

2 When the pastry is big enough to cover a 25 cm pie plate, lift it on to the rolling pin and lay it flat on the plate.

3 Press it into place and cut off any extra pastry. Lightly prick the bottom with a fork but try not to prick right through.

4 Put 8 tablespoons of golden syrup into a saucepan. Add the lemon zest, juice and a pinch of ginger, then heat gently.

5 Pour half the syrup on to the pastry then sprinkle over half the breadcrumbs. Add the rest of the syrup and crumbs.

6 Decorate the edge of the pastry by making small cuts all the way round the edge and folding down as illustrated.

7 Put the tart on a baking sheet and bake for 30 minutes until the pastry is golden brown and the filling a little soft.

Pavlova

This is a very easy meringue to make and it tastes lovely if it is still rather soft in the middle.

You will need:
4 egg whites (see page 13)
pinch of salt
200 g caster sugar
1 teaspoon cornflour
1 teaspoon vanilla essence
1 teaspoon lemon juice
142 ml carton double cream
150 g low fat natural yogurt
a mixture of about 500 g of your favourite fresh fruits

Preheat the oven to Gas Mark 1, 140°C or 275°F

1 Prepare a baking sheet by covering it with a piece of baking parchment or silicone paper.

2 Put the egg whites into a large, very clean, dry mixing bowl and place the bowl on a damp cloth to stop it slipping.

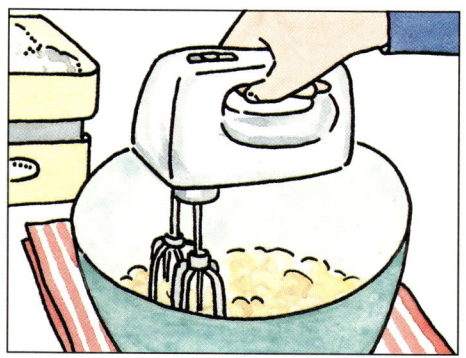

3 Add the salt and using an electric mixer whisk until stiff. Add the sugar gradually, whisking until very stiff.

4 Stir in the cornflour, vanilla essence and lemon juice. Spoon on to the baking sheet and shape into a 3 cm deep circle.

5 Bake the Pavlova for about 1 hour. The meringue is cooked when it looks pale brown and is hard to touch.

6 Remove the baking sheet from the oven and leave the meringue to cool. Peel the paper off when completely cold.

7 Put the cream into a bowl and whisk until thick. Add the yogurt and fold it into the cream with a spoon.

8 Spread the cream and yogurt over the cold meringue and arrange the fruit over the top of the cream.

Variations:
You can use any fruits you like on a Pavlova. We used fresh ripe strawberries, raspberries and plums, but you could try kiwi fruits, mangoes, redcurrants, nectarines or grapes and decorate with mint leaves.